What is a Growth Mindset?

Embrace the power of growth and learning

Anthony Mondragon

Table of Contents

Chapter 3: Embracing Challenges (25)

- The Importance of Embracing Challenges for Developing a Growth Mindset
- Understanding and Overcoming the Fear of Failure
- Reframing Challenges as Opportunities for Growth

Chapter 4: Cultivating Resilience (34)

- The Power of Resilience in Developing a Growth Mindset
- Strategies for Bouncing Back and Overcoming Obstacles
- Practicing Self-Compassion: Treating Ourselves with Kindness During Difficult Times
- Seeking Support: Building a Strong Network of Encouragement

Chapter 5: The Role of Effort and Practice (45)

- Understanding the Significance of Effort and Deliberate Practice in Developing Skills
- Embracing the Process of Improvement and Setting Clear Goals
- Cultivating Growth Mindset Practices

Pre Introduction

I chose to write this book because I have been on my own impactful personal journey of growth and self-improvement. I wanted to find a way to share the powerful insights and lessons that have helped transform my mindset, in the hopes they may support others in their development.

My core goal was to create something genuinely uplifting that provides value for people seeking guidance, clarity and direction. The concepts in this book come straight from my personal path of growth. They reflect my heartfelt desire to illuminate the way for others.

To bring this book to life, I decided to collaborate with an AI writing assistant. My sole intention was to create the best possible book I could in order to spread knowledge that could help people. The AI helped me organize my thoughts, conduct supplementary research, refine explanations, and articulate the ideas in a more resonant way.

The motivation and inspiration comes directly from my own journey. However, partnering with AI enabled me to produce a book that was far richer than I could have created alone. But the essence remains true to my purpose.

My hope is that this book provides inspiration, wisdom and practical tools that you can apply to your own path of growth and self-discovery. If I can impart some clarity and light that helps orient you on your personal development journey, then I have accomplished my goal.

I am honored to share this knowledge from my ongoing experience - one seeker to another. May your path lead you to your highest potentials!

Introduction

Welcome to "What is a Growth Mindset?" In this book, we will embark on a transformative journey to explore the power of growth and learning. By diving into the concept of a growth mindset, we aim to uncover the incredible potential that lies within each of us to develop, adapt, and thrive. Have you ever wondered why some people seem to effortlessly overcome challenges and achieve great things while others struggle to make progress? The answer lies in their mindset. Our mindset, the set of beliefs and attitudes we hold about ourselves and our abilities, plays a crucial role in determining our success, happiness, and fulfillment in life.

In this fast-paced and ever-changing world, cultivating a growth mindset is more important than ever. It is a mindset that embraces challenges, sees failures as opportunities for growth, and believes in the power of effort, practice, and continuous learning. With a growth mindset, we can navigate obstacles, overcome self-doubt, and unlock our true potential. Throughout the pages of this book, we will explore the key elements of a growth mindset and how they can profoundly impact every aspect of our lives. Drawing from extensive research, I will provide you with practical strategies and insights to adopt and nurture a growth mindset.

By understanding the differences between a fixed mindset and a growth mindset, you will gain valuable insights into your own beliefs and thought patterns. You will discover how these mindsets shape your behavior, emotions, and ultimately, the outcomes you experience. With this awareness, you can make conscious choices to shift towards a growth mindset and unlock new levels of personal and professional growth. But this book is not just about personal transformation; it's also about fostering a growth mindset in others. Whether you are a parent, educator, or leader, you have the power to influence and nurture the growth mindset of those around you. We will explore practical strategies to create environments that encourage learning, development, and resilience. Are you ready to embark on this enlightening journey of self-discovery and growth? Together, we will challenge our beliefs, embrace setbacks, and cultivate the mindset needed to thrive in an ever-changing world. Get ready to unlock your potential and embrace the power of growth and learning.

In the chapters that follow, we will dive into the core principles of a growth mindset, examining the role of beliefs, the importance of embracing challenges, the significance of effort and practice, and the value of learning and feedback. We will also explore how to nurture a growth mindset in others, empowering them to reach new heights. So, let's begin our exploration of "What is a Growth Mindset?" and discover the incredible opportunities that await us when we embrace the power of growth and learning.

As we dive into each chapter, you may notice recurring themes and overlapping ideas. While this may seem repetitive, it serves a crucial purpose repetition reinforces essential concepts and allows them to take root in your mind. Embracing a growth mindset requires continuous reminders and practice. The more we immerse ourselves in the principles of growth, resilience, and self-improvement, the more deeply they become ingrained in our thinking and behaviors. So, embrace the repetition as a powerful tool in shaping your mindset and unleashing your true potential. Let's dive in and discover the life-changing possibilities that a growth mindset can bring.Next, we will delve into

Chapter 1: Understanding Mindsets, where we will differentiate between a fixed mindset and a growth mindset, exploring the research and real-life examples that illustrate their impact.

Chapter 1:

Understanding Mindsets

In this chapter, we will explore the significance of mindsets in shaping our thoughts, behaviors, and outcomes. We will highlight the transformative power of adopting a growth mindset and dive into the differences between a fixed mindset and a growth mindset.

The Fixed Mindset vs. The Growth Mindset
Mindsets play a crucial role in how we perceive and navigate the world. A fixed mindset is characterized by the belief that our abilities and intelligence are fixed traits. In contrast, a growth mindset is based on the belief that our abilities can be developed through effort, learning, and perseverance.

Differentiating between the fixed mindset and the growth mindset helps us understand their impact on our lives. The fixed mindset is associated with beliefs that our qualities are predetermined and unchangeable. It often leads to avoiding challenges, fearing failure, and viewing setbacks as personal limitations. On the other hand, the growth mindset embraces challenges, sees failure as an opportunity for growth, and believes in the power of effort and learning.

Understanding these mindsets allows us to recognize how they influence our approach to challenges, learning, and personal development. The fixed mindset can hinder growth and limit our potential, while the growth mindset empowers us to embrace challenges, persist in the face of setbacks, and continuously improve.

The Fixed Mindset

The fixed mindset is characterized by the belief that our abilities and intelligence are fixed traits, determined at birth, and unchangeable. Individuals with a fixed mindset tend to view their qualities as predetermined, leading to a rigid perspective on their potential and limitations. They often avoid challenges and fear failure, perceiving them as threats to their sense of competence. Failure confirms their belief in their limited abilities, which hinders their willingness to take risks and explore new opportunities.

Those with a fixed mindset focus on maintaining their image of competence rather than on growth and improvement. They seek validation and praise from others, relying on external feedback to reinforce their sense of self-worth. Setbacks and failures are interpreted as personal limitations, leading to a diminished sense of self-confidence.

People with a fixed mindset resist effort and change. They may believe that if they need to exert effort, it means they lack natural talent or intelligence. They prefer to stick to what they already know and are comfortable with, limiting their growth and potential for development.

Understanding the characteristics of the fixed mindset allows us to recognize these tendencies within ourselves and others. By becoming aware of our fixed mindset tendencies, we can actively work towards adopting a growth mindset, which we will explore further in the next chapters.

The Growth Mindset

The growth mindset is based on the belief that our abilities and intelligence can be developed through dedication, effort, and continuous learning. Individuals with a growth mindset exhibit a set of characteristics that shape their approach to challenges, learning, and personal development. People with a growth mindset embrace challenges and persist in the face of setbacks. They see challenges as opportunities for growth and learning, understanding that by stepping out of their comfort zone and embracing challenges, they can expand their abilities, develop new skills, and gain valuable experiences. They persevere through obstacles and setbacks, recognizing that these are natural parts of the learning process.

In contrast to viewing failure as a source of discouragement, those with a growth mindset see failure as a stepping stone to success. They view setbacks as valuable feedback that guides them toward improvement. Rather than being discouraged by failure, they use it as an opportunity to learn, adjust their strategies, and approach future attempts with increased knowledge and experience.

Individuals with a growth mindset value effort, learning, and continuous improvement. They understand the importance of dedication and hard work in developing their skills and intelligence. They believe that with ongoing effort and deliberate practice, they can enhance their abilities and achieve their goals. They embrace the idea that lifelong learning and personal growth are essential for reaching their full potential.

Seeking feedback and learning from others is another key characteristic of those with a growth mindset. They actively seek feedback from others, recognizing it as a valuable source of information that can help them identify areas for improvement. They are open to constructive criticism and use it to refine their skills, enhance their performance, and accelerate their growth.

Understanding and adopting a growth mindset empowers individuals to embrace their potential, cultivate resilience, and continuously develop their abilities.

Chapter2:

The Power of Beliefs

In this chapter, we will explore the role of beliefs in shaping our mindset and influencing our thoughts, behaviors, and outcomes. We will examine the impact of self-perception, self-talk, and external influences on our beliefs and mindset. Additionally, we will provide strategies for identifying and challenging limiting beliefs to foster a growth mindset.

Self-Perception and Self-Talk: Shaping Our Mindset

Our self-perception and the language we use in our self-talk play a crucial role in shaping our mindset. The beliefs we hold about ourselves and our abilities can either support or hinder our growth. If we have negative or limiting beliefs about our capabilities, it can hinder our progress and limit our potential. Therefore, it is important to become aware of our self-perception and the messages we repeatedly tell ourselves.

Cultivating self-awareness is the first step in understanding our self-perception. By paying attention to our thoughts, emotions, and beliefs, we can gain insights into how we perceive ourselves. Take a moment to reflect on the beliefs you hold about your abilities. Are there any self-limiting beliefs that hold you back? Are there areas where you underestimate your potential? Becoming aware of these beliefs is crucial for transforming our mindset.

Once we identify negative or self-defeating thoughts and beliefs, we can challenge and reframe them to support a growth mindset. This process involves consciously replacing negative self-talk with positive and empowering statements that reinforce our ability to learn, grow, and overcome challenges. For example, instead of saying, "I'm not good at this,"
we can reframe it as, "I am capable of learning and improving in this area with effort and practice." By consciously choosing to shift our self-talk, we

create an internal dialogue that supports our growth and development.

Affirmations can be powerful tools for reshaping our self-perception and self-talk. Affirmations are positive statements that we repeat to ourselves to reinforce positive beliefs and attitudes. By regularly reciting affirmations that align with a growth mindset, such as "I embrace challenges as opportunities for growth" or "I am resilient and capable of overcoming obstacles," we program our minds to embrace a growth-oriented perspective.

In addition to affirmations, it is important to surround ourselves with positive influences and supportive individuals who reinforce a growth mindset. Seek out mentors, friends, or colleagues who embody a growth mindset and can provide encouragement, guidance, and constructive feedback. Engage in communities or join groups that share your values of growth and development. By surrounding ourselves with like-minded individuals, we create a supportive environment that nurtures our growth mindset.

Remember, our self-perception and self-talk are not fixed. They can be transformed through self-awareness, intentional reframing, and consistent practice. By cultivating a positive and empowering self-perception, we open ourselves up to new possibilities and unleash our true potential.

External Influences: The Power of Surroundings
Our mindset is not solely shaped by our internal beliefs; external influences also play a significant role. The opinions and expectations of others, societal norms, and cultural influences can impact our mindset and shape our beliefs about ourselves and our potential. It is important to be mindful of these external influences and their potential to either support or hinder our growth mindset.

The people we surround ourselves with can greatly influence our mindset. By actively choosing our surroundings and seeking out positive and growth-oriented individuals, we can create an environment that supports and nurtures our growth mindset. Surrounding ourselves with people who believe in our potential and encourage us to embrace challenges can have a profound impact on our mindset and foster our personal development. These individuals can provide valuable support, inspiration, and accountability as we navigate our growth journey.

In addition to the people we surround ourselves with, the environments we immerse ourselves in also contribute to our mindset. The places we frequent, such as our workplace, educational institutions, or social circles, can shape our beliefs and attitudes. It is important to evaluate whether these environments foster a growth mindset or a fixed mindset. If we find ourselves in environments that discourage growth and limit our potential, it may be beneficial to seek out alternative settings that align with our growth-oriented values.

Cultural and societal influences can also impact our mindset. Societal norms, expectations, and pressures can shape our beliefs about success, failure, and personal growth. It is important to critically examine these influences and question whether they align with our own values and aspirations. By challenging societal norms that may reinforce a fixed mindset, we can create space for personal growth and pave the way for a more expansive mindset.

Ultimately, we have the power to shape our surroundings and intentionally choose the influences that align with our growth mindset. By surrounding ourselves with individuals and environments that foster positivity, support growth, and encourage us to embrace challenges, we create a fertile ground for our personal and professional development. It is through this deliberate selection of external influences that we can reinforce and nourish our growth mindset.

Challenging Limiting Beliefs: Shifting Perspectives

In the journey towards developing a growth mindset, one of the most critical steps is to confront and challenge our limiting beliefs. Limiting beliefs are deeply ingrained assumptions about ourselves and the world around us that hinder our progress and personal growth. These beliefs can act as invisible barriers, preventing us from realizing our full potential.

To foster a growth mindset, it is essential to identify these limiting beliefs and actively challenge their validity. We often inherit these beliefs from past experiences, cultural influences, or negative feedback from others. However, we have the power to rewrite the narratives that shape our self-perception.

The process of challenging limiting beliefs involves questioning the accuracy and impact of these beliefs on our lives. We can ask ourselves: Are these beliefs based on objective evidence, or are they simply assumptions or interpretations? How do these beliefs affect our behavior and decisions? What opportunities or aspirations do we avoid due to these beliefs? Are there alternative perspectives that could empower us to overcome these limitations?

By bringing these limiting beliefs to light, we gain the opportunity to reframe and shift our perspective. We replace self-defeating thoughts with empowering ones that align with a growth mindset.

For example, if we hold the limiting belief that we are "not good enough" to pursue a particular career path, we can challenge it by seeking evidence of our strengths, skills, and past achievements. We can remind ourselves of the times when we demonstrated competence and determination in other areas of our lives. By recognizing our potential for growth and improvement, we open ourselves up to new possibilities and opportunities.

Cultivating a growth mindset involves cultivating a positive and constructive inner dialogue. When we encounter challenges, we can replace negative self-talk with affirmations that reinforce our ability to learn, adapt, and overcome obstacles. By practicing self-compassion and offering ourselves encouragement, we build a foundation of resilience that supports our growth journey.

It is essential to recognize that challenging limiting beliefs is an ongoing process. As we encounter new challenges and opportunities, new limiting beliefs may surface. However, by cultivating self-awareness and a commitment to growth, we equip ourselves with the tools needed to challenge these beliefs continually.

In this chapter, we explored the influence of self-perception, external surroundings, and challenging limiting beliefs on shaping our mindset. Our self-perception and self-talk play a crucial role in determining our beliefs about our abilities. By cultivating self-awareness and shifting our perspective, we can challenge limiting beliefs and embrace a growth mindset. External influences, such as societal norms and the opinions of others, also impact our mindset. However, we can choose positive surroundings that foster a growth-oriented perspective.

As we continue our journey towards a growth mindset, let us remain mindful of our beliefs' power and embrace the transformative potential they hold. In the upcoming chapters, we'll delve into practical strategies and practices to further reinforce our growth mindset and flourish in a world of endless possibilities.

Chapter 3:

Embracing Challenges

In this chapter, we will explore the significance of embracing challenges in developing a growth mindset. We will discuss the fear of failure and its impact on our mindset, as well as provide techniques for reframing challenges as opportunities for growth.

The Importance of Embracing Challenges
Embracing challenges is crucial for developing a growth mindset. Challenges provide opportunities for us to stretch our abilities, learn new skills, and expand our comfort zones. By actively seeking out challenges, we can cultivate resilience, enhance our problem-solving skills, and foster a mindset that embraces continuous growth.

Embracing challenges is not only an integral part of personal growth but also a key factor in developing a growth mindset. Challenges provide us with opportunities to stretch our abilities, learn new skills, and expand our comfort zones. They push us beyond our current limits and help us discover our true potential.

When we actively seek out challenges, we cultivate resilience within ourselves. By willingly stepping outside of our comfort zones, we develop the ability to adapt and bounce back from setbacks. We become more adept at navigating obstacles and finding creative solutions. Each challenge we encounter becomes a chance to strengthen our problem-solving skills and enhance our ability to overcome adversity.

Embracing challenges fosters a mindset that is oriented toward continuous growth. Rather than fearing failure or avoiding difficult tasks, we approach them with curiosity and determination. We understand that challenges are not indicators of our limitations but opportunities for growth and learning. By embracing challenges, we cultivate a belief in our own capacity to learn, adapt, and improve.

It is important to note that challenges come in different forms and can vary in magnitude. They can be professional, personal, or academic in nature. Embracing challenges is not about seeking unnecessary hardships but rather about recognizing the value they bring to our personal and professional development. It's about pushing ourselves to go beyond what is comfortable and familiar, knowing that growth lies on the other side of our comfort zones.

As we actively embrace challenges, we become more resilient, adaptable, and open to new experiences. We discover that our potential is not fixed, but rather expandable with effort and dedication. By viewing challenges as opportunities for growth, we foster a growth mindset that propels us forward on our journey of continuous development.

Remember, the path to personal growth is paved with challenges. Embrace them as stepping stones on your journey. Each challenge you encounter is an opportunity to unlock new capabilities and discover the heights of your potential. Embracing challenges is not always easy, but the rewards are immeasurable. It is through these challenges that we truly thrive and cultivate a growth mindset that propels us toward greater achievements.

Understanding the Fear of Failure

The fear of failure often acts as a formidable barrier to embracing challenges and developing a growth mindset. It stems from the belief that failure is a reflection of our inadequacy and limitations. We are conditioned to view failure as something to be avoided at all costs, fearing the judgment and criticism that may accompany it. However, it is essential to recognize that failure is not a verdict on our worth or capabilities. Instead, it is an integral part of the learning process and an opportunity for growth.

To overcome the fear of failure, we must reframe our perception of it. Rather than seeing failure as a personal defeat, we can choose to view it as a valuable feedback mechanism. Each failure provides us with insights and lessons that can guide our future endeavors. It illuminates the areas where we can improve, adjust our strategies, and expand our knowledge and skills. When we approach failure with a growth mindset, we recognize its inherent value in our personal and professional development.

It is important to shift our focus from the fear of failure to the fear of not trying at all. The regret of not taking action and missing out on potential growth opportunities can outweigh the fear of failure itself. By reframing failure as a necessary stepping stone toward success, we can embrace challenges with a sense of courage and determination.

Overcoming the fear of failure requires a mindset shift. We must recognize that failure does not define us, but rather, it provides us with valuable feedback and insights for improvement. By cultivating a growth mindset, we understand that our abilities are not fixed, but can be developed through effort and learning. With this mindset, we can approach challenges with resilience and view failure as an essential part of the journey toward achieving our goals.

Remember, failure is not the end; it is a stepping stone on the path to growth. Embrace the fear of not trying and choose to face challenges head-on. By reframing failure as an opportunity for growth, you unlock your true potential and pave the way for greater achievements.

Reframing Challenges as Opportunities for Growth

To develop a growth mindset, it is essential to reframe challenges as opportunities for growth rather than threats to our self-worth. Challenges are not obstacles to be avoided, but valuable experiences that push us outside our comfort zones and stimulate our personal and professional development. By shifting our perspective, we can view challenges as stepping stones that help us develop new skills, expand our knowledge, and build resilience.

When we reframe challenges, we approach them with a sense of curiosity and enthusiasm. We see them as opportunities to stretch ourselves and discover untapped potential. Instead of fearing failure or doubting our abilities, we embrace the process of learning and growth that comes with facing challenges head-on. We understand that the greatest growth occurs when we step outside our comfort zones and confront new and unfamiliar situations.

Reframing challenges allows us to believe in our ability to learn and improve. Rather than being discouraged by setbacks or obstacles, we see them as opportunities to learn from our mistakes and adjust our strategies. Each challenge becomes a chance to develop new skills, acquire knowledge, and hone our problem-solving abilities. We approach challenges with a growth mindset, understanding that the process of overcoming them is just as important as the outcome itself.

By reframing challenges, we build resilience. We develop the capacity to bounce back from setbacks and persevere in the face of adversity. Challenges become catalysts for personal growth, strengthening our confidence, and nurturing our ability to navigate future obstacles with greater ease. With each challenge overcome, we gain confidence in our ability to tackle new and increasingly complex situations.

Remember, challenges are not roadblocks; they are opportunities for growth. Embrace them with a mindset of curiosity, enthusiasm, and a belief in your ability to learn and improve. Reframe challenges as valuable experiences that propel you forward on your journey of personal and professional development. By shifting your perspective, you open yourself up to endless possibilities and unlock your true potential.

Techniques for Embracing Challenges
In this section, we will explore practical techniques for embracing challenges and cultivating a growth mindset. First, setting stretch goals is an effective approach. By setting goals that push us outside our comfort zones, we encourage personal growth and foster a mindset focused on continuous improvement. These goals provide opportunities to develop new skills, expand our knowledge, and overcome obstacles along the way.

Second, adopting a learning orientation is crucial. Emphasizing the process of learning and growth, rather than solely focusing on outcomes, helps us maintain a positive mindset and view setbacks as opportunities for improvement. It allows us to appreciate the value of the learning journey and the lessons we gain from facing challenges.

Third, cultivating resilience is essential for embracing challenges. Developing resilience enables us to bounce back from setbacks and persevere in the face of obstacles. Techniques such as reframing challenges, practicing self-compassion, and seeking support can help build resilience, empowering us to stay motivated and resilient in the face of difficulties.

Lastly, embracing a growth mindset language plays a significant role. Using language that reflects a growth mindset, such as "yet" and "not yet," reinforces the belief that abilities can be developed over time. This language encourages a positive approach to challenges, reminding us that we are constantly learning and evolving.

Chapter 4:

Cultivating Resilience

In this chapter, we will explore the importance of resilience in developing a growth mindset. We will highlight the significance of bouncing back from setbacks and overcoming obstacles, and share strategies for cultivating resilience to foster personal growth and success.

The Power of Resilience
Resilience is a potent force that fuels our growth mindset and empowers us to face life's challenges with unwavering determination. It is the ability to bounce back from adversity, setbacks, and failures, emerging stronger and more determined to pursue our goals. Resilience acts as a guiding light during tough times, allowing us to maintain a positive attitude and view obstacles as stepping stones on our journey to success.

The key characteristic of resilience is its ability to help us persevere even in the face of difficulties. Resilient individuals maintain a sense of hope and optimism, believing that setbacks are temporary and surmountable. They see challenges as opportunities for growth and learning, rather than insurmountable roadblocks. This unwavering faith in their ability to overcome obstacles is what differentiates resilient individuals from those who succumb to adversity.

When we cultivate resilience, we develop a deep inner strength that propels us forward, no matter the circumstances. Resilience allows us to maintain focus on our goals and stay committed to our vision, even when the path becomes uncertain or arduous. It fosters an unshakeable belief in our potential and the knowledge that every challenge is an opportunity for growth.

Moreover, resilience helps us navigate through life's inevitable ups and downs with grace and courage. It equips us with the mental and emotional tools to cope with stress and uncertainty, allowing us to adapt to change and face challenges head-on.

Resilient individuals remain flexible and open to new possibilities, understanding that change brings opportunities for growth and self-discovery.

Resilience is not an innate trait reserved for a select few; rather, it is a skill that can be developed and strengthened over time. By consciously practicing resilience, we can cultivate a growth mindset that fuels our personal and professional development. Embracing challenges, seeking support, and practicing self-compassion are some of the key strategies for nurturing resilience.

In the following sections, we will explore practical strategies for building resilience and bouncing back from setbacks. By adopting these approaches, we can harness the power of resilience to overcome obstacles, maintain our growth mindset, and forge ahead on the path to success.

Reframing and Perspective Shifts

In the pursuit of a growth mindset, the practice of reframing setbacks and adopting perspective shifts becomes a transformative force. Resilient individuals recognize that setbacks and failures are not dead-ends but valuable learning opportunities. Rather than seeing challenges as insurmountable roadblocks, they reframe them as stepping stones on their path to personal growth and success.

When faced with adversity, resilient individuals consciously choose to interpret setbacks differently. They shift their perspective from a fixed mindset that views failure as a confirmation of their limitations, to a growth mindset that understands failure as a natural part of the learning process. By adopting this mindset, they transform challenges from daunting obstacles into powerful catalysts for self-improvement.

To cultivate this ability, it is essential to develop self-awareness and monitor our internal dialogue. When we encounter setbacks, we can ask ourselves critical questions: What can I learn from this experience? How can I use this feedback to refine my approach? What steps can I take to progress further?

By asking these questions, we begin to see setbacks as sources of valuable feedback rather than personal shortcomings. Reframing challenges in this way encourages us to embrace the growth mindset, where our focus shifts from seeking validation for our abilities to seeking opportunities for continuous learning and development.

In the process of reframing setbacks, we also learn to let go of self-limiting beliefs and embrace a growth-oriented perspective. Resilient individuals understand that success is not a linear path, but a series of iterations and improvements. They recognize that setbacks are an inherent part of any journey towards excellence and that each setback brings with it the potential for growth and self-discovery.

Through the practice of reframing, we build resilience that becomes the bedrock of our growth mindset. We learn to approach challenges with enthusiasm, curiosity, and an unwavering belief in our capacity to learn and evolve. By transforming setbacks into stepping stones for growth, we foster a mindset that enables us to take on new challenges with courage and optimism, unlocking our true potential and propelling us towards success.

Practicing Self-Compassion

Self-compassion involves treating ourselves with kindness, understanding, and acceptance during difficult times. By being compassionate towards ourselves, we can bounce back from setbacks with resilience. Self-compassion allows us to acknowledge our emotions, learn from our mistakes, and use setbacks as stepping stones toward personal growth.

When we encounter difficulties or experience failures, our natural response may be self-criticism and self-blame. However, resilient individuals choose self-compassion instead. They understand that self-criticism is counterproductive and only serves to deepen negative emotions, leading to a spiral of self-doubt and fear.

Embracing self-compassion begins with recognizing and acknowledging our emotions without judgment. We allow ourselves to feel the disappointment, frustration, or sadness that may arise from setbacks, understanding that these emotions are a natural part of the human experience.

Next, we offer ourselves words of kindness and encouragement, just as we would offer comfort to a friend facing a difficult situation. Rather than berating ourselves for our perceived shortcomings, we reassure ourselves that setbacks are an inherent part of growth and that failures do not define our worth or potential.

Furthermore, practicing self-compassion involves recognizing our shared humanity. We remind ourselves that everyone faces challenges and setbacks, and we are not alone in experiencing difficulties. This understanding fosters a sense of common humanity, breaking the isolation that setbacks can sometimes create.

Through self-compassion, we cultivate an inner ally—a voice that is supportive, nurturing, and understanding. This ally helps us bounce back from setbacks with resilience and optimism, as it reminds us that we are deserving of kindness, love, and forgiveness, regardless of our achievements or failures.

Moreover, self-compassion allows us to learn and grow from setbacks rather than avoiding them out of fear of failure. When we are compassionate towards ourselves, we are more willing to take risks and explore new possibilities, knowing that we are supported, no matter the outcome.

By embracing self-compassion, we build a foundation of emotional resilience that empowers us to face challenges with grace and courage. It becomes a key component of our growth mindset, fostering an environment where learning, self-improvement, and personal development can thrive.

Seeking Support

In our journey towards cultivating resilience and fostering a growth mindset, seeking support becomes a crucial element. Building a resilient network of family, friends, mentors, or coaches provides us with a safety net during challenging times and offers valuable encouragement and guidance to navigate through setbacks.

One of the fundamental aspects of seeking support is recognizing that we do not have to face our challenges alone. By sharing our experiences and seeking guidance from trusted individuals, we gain new perspectives and insights that can help us overcome obstacles more effectively.

When seeking support, it is essential to surround ourselves with positive and growth-oriented individuals who believe in our potential. These supportive individuals understand the importance of embracing challenges and view setbacks as opportunities for growth, just like we do.
A strong support system can provide the emotional reinforcement needed to bounce back from setbacks with resilience. When we face challenges, having someone who believes in us and reminds us of our strengths can be a powerful motivator. Their encouragement can renew our sense of purpose and commitment to our growth journey.

Moreover, seeking support allows us to tap into the wisdom and experience of others. Mentors and coaches, in particular, can offer valuable guidance and advice based on their own journeys and expertise. Learning from those who have faced similar challenges and overcome them instills hope and provides a roadmap for our growth.

In addition to the emotional and practical support, being part of a resilient network nurtures a sense of belonging and connection. Knowing that we are not alone in our struggles creates a sense of common humanity, which can be profoundly comforting during difficult times.

It is important to be proactive in seeking support and fostering meaningful relationships with individuals who share our growth mindset values. Engaging in communities, workshops, or online groups focused on personal development can be a valuable way to connect with like-minded individuals.

By actively building a resilient network, we create an environment that nurtures our growth mindset and empowers us to face challenges with strength and determination. Our support system becomes a source of encouragement, guidance, and perspective that helps us cultivate resilience and navigate obstacles on our path to success.

Cultivating Growth Mindset practices
Practicing growth mindset principles, such as embracing challenges, valuing effort, and maintaining a positive attitude, strengthens our resilience. By approaching challenges as opportunities for growth, persisting in the face of setbacks, and believing in our ability to improve, we can foster resilience and continue to grow despite difficulties.

In this chapter, we explored the importance of cultivating resilience in developing a growth mindset. Resilience allows us to bounce back from setbacks, maintain a positive attitude, and view challenges as opportunities for growth.

Chapter 5:

The Role of Effort and Practice

In this chapter, we will explore the significance of effort and practice in developing a growth mindset. We will discuss the importance of deliberate practice, setting goals, and implementing effective strategies to achieve our desired outcomes.

The Power of Effort, Deliberate Practice, and Goal Setting

Effort and deliberate practice are key factors in developing a growth mindset. While natural talent may provide a foundation, it is the consistent effort and deliberate practice that lead to mastery. By understanding the power of effort, we can cultivate a mindset that values hard work, persistence, and continuous improvement.

Setting goals is an essential aspect of developing a growth mindset. Goals provide direction and focus, motivating us to take action and strive for improvement. By setting meaningful goals, we create a roadmap for our growth and development. It is important to set specific, measurable, achievable, relevant, and time-bound (SMART) goals that challenge us and push us beyond our comfort zones. These goals serve as milestones along our journey, allowing us to track our progress and celebrate our achievements. Through the process of setting goals, we enhance our motivation, clarify our vision, and create a sense of purpose in our pursuit of personal growth.

By combining effort, deliberate practice, and goal setting, we create a powerful framework for developing skills and fostering a growth mindset. The commitment to consistent effort and deliberate practice, coupled with the focus provided by goal setting, propels us forward on our path of continuous improvement and development.

Implementing Effective Practice Strategies
Practice is crucial for skill development and personal growth. In this section, we will discuss effective practice strategies that can help us

maximize our learning and progress. One important strategy is breaking tasks into manageable parts. By breaking down larger goals into smaller, more achievable tasks, we can maintain focus, build momentum, and track our progress more effectively. Additionally, seeking feedback from knowledgeable individuals can provide valuable insights and help us identify areas for improvement. Feedback allows us to fine-tune our skills and make necessary adjustments along the way.

Reflection is another powerful practice strategy. Taking time to reflect on our performance, whether it's after completing a task or at regular intervals, allows us to gain deeper insights into our strengths, weaknesses, and areas of growth. By analyzing our experiences and learning from both successes and failures, we can make more informed decisions, refine our strategies, and continuously improve.

Incorporating deliberate practice techniques is also key. Deliberate practice involves intentionally focusing on areas that require improvement, pushing ourselves beyond our comfort zones, and engaging in targeted, purposeful practice. By identifying specific aspects of our skills or knowledge that need attention and creating structured practice sessions to address them, we can accelerate our progress and enhance our growth mindset.

Embracing the Growth Mindset in the Learning Process

A growth mindset is particularly valuable when it comes to learning. By embracing a growth mindset in our educational pursuits, we approach challenges with curiosity, view mistakes as learning opportunities, and

recognize that intelligence can be developed. Adopting a growth mindset allows us to overcome the fear of failure and take risks in our learning journey. We understand that setbacks are temporary and serve as valuable feedback for improvement. Furthermore, a growth mindset fosters motivation and resilience in the face of challenges. We maintain a belief that with effort, practice, and effective strategies, we can continually expand our knowledge and skills. By adopting a growth mindset, we become more open to seeking help, collaborating with others, and embracing the joy of lifelong learning.

In this chapter, we explored the role of effort and practice in developing a growth mindset. We discussed the power of effort, deliberate practice, and goal setting in fostering continuous improvement and skill development. By implementing effective practice strategies, such as breaking tasks into manageable parts, seeking feedback, reflecting on our performance, and incorporating deliberate practice techniques, we enhance our learning and skill acquisition. Embracing a growth mindset in the learning process enables us to approach challenges with curiosity, view mistakes as learning opportunities, and maintain motivation and resilience.

In the next chapter, we will dive into the importance of embracing learning and feedback as essential components of a growth mindset.

Chapter 6:

Embrace Learning and Feedback

In this chapter, we will explore the importance of embracing learning and feedback as essential components of a growth mindset. We will discuss how adopting a mindset that values continuous learning and seeks feedback can enhance personal growth, development, and achievement.

The Value of Continuous Learning and The Power of Seeking Feedback

Continuous learning is a cornerstone of a growth mindset. Embracing a mindset that values learning allows us to approach new challenges with enthusiasm and curiosity. It encourages us to see each experience as an opportunity to expand our knowledge, acquire new skills, and explore different perspectives. By adopting a commitment to continuous learning, we acknowledge that there is always room for improvement and growth. We actively seek out opportunities to broaden our horizons and enhance our understanding of the world around us.

Seeking feedback is a powerful practice that contributes to our growth and development. Feedback provides valuable insights into our strengths, areas for improvement, and blind spots. By actively seeking feedback from trusted sources, such as mentors, colleagues, or teachers, we gain a deeper understanding of our abilities and how we can enhance them. Constructive feedback helps us identify areas for growth, adjust our strategies, and make necessary improvements. It allows us to gain different perspectives, challenge our assumptions, and expand our thinking. When we embrace feedback as a valuable tool for personal and professional development, we open ourselves up to continuous improvement and growth.

By combining the value of continuous learning and the power of seeking feedback, we create a powerful framework for personal growth and development. Embracing a growth mindset that values continuous learning and seeks feedback allows us to continually evolve, adapt, and excel in various areas of our lives.

The Benefits of a Growth Mindset in the Learning Process

Embracing a growth mindset in the learning process has numerous benefits. When we approach learning with a growth mindset, we believe that intelligence and abilities can be developed through effort, practice, and effective strategies. This belief fuels our motivation and perseverance in the face of challenges. We view setbacks as opportunities for learning and growth, rather than as indications of our limitations. By embracing a growth mindset, we are more likely to take risks, embrace new challenges, and persist in our pursuit of knowledge and skills.

Effective Approaches to Learning and Feedback

Developing a Reflective Practice:

Engaging in reflection allows us to consolidate our learning, identify areas for improvement, and make meaning from our experiences. Reflection can take various forms, such as journaling, self-assessment, or engaging in meaningful conversations.

Implementing Actionable Feedback:
When receiving feedback, it is essential to approach it with an open mind and a willingness to learn and grow. Actively listen, ask clarifying questions, and identify actionable steps to incorporate the feedback into our practice.

Creating a Supportive Learning Environment:
Fostering a supportive learning environment, whether it's in a classroom, workplace, or personal setting, encourages collaboration, open dialogue, and constructive feedback. Creating
a culture that values learning and supports growth mindset principles enhances the learning experience for everyone involved.

In this chapter, we explored the importance of embracing learning and feedback as essential components of a growth mindset. Continuous learning allows us to expand our knowledge and skills, while seeking feedback provides valuable insights for growth and improvement. By adopting a growth mindset in the learning process, we approach challenges with enthusiasm, view setbacks as opportunities for growth, and persist in our pursuit of knowledge and personal development. In the next chapter, we will discuss the importance of nurturing a growth mindset in others and explore strategies for fostering a growth mindset in children, students, and team members.

Chapter 7:

Nurturing a Growth Mindset in Others

In this chapter, we will explore the role of parents, teachers, leaders, and individuals in fostering a growth mindset in others. We will discuss strategies for creating a supportive environment that encourages the development of a growth mindset in children, students, and team members.

The Influence of Parents and Caregivers
Parents and caregivers play a significant role in shaping the mindset of children. By modeling a growth mindset and providing encouragement and support, parents can foster a belief in the power of effort, learning, and growth. One effective strategy is to praise effort and persistence rather than focusing solely on outcomes. By acknowledging and praising the process of learning and the effort invested, parents can instill in children the understanding that hard work and dedication lead to

growth and improvement. Additionally, emphasizing the importance of learning from mistakes and setbacks helps children develop resilience and a willingness to take on challenges.

Creating opportunities for learning and exploration is another essential aspect of fostering a growth mindset in children. Providing a stimulating environment with diverse resources, encouraging curiosity, and supporting their interests and passions allow children to develop a love for learning and a growth-oriented mindset. By nurturing a supportive and encouraging atmosphere at home, parents and caregivers can help children develop the confidence to take risks, embrace challenges, and persist in their pursuit of knowledge and personal growth.

Fostering a Growth Mindset in Education

Educators have a unique opportunity to foster a growth mindset in students. By creating a classroom environment that values effort, encourages risk-taking, and provides opportunities for growth, teachers can inspire a love for learning and nurture the belief that abilities can be developed. One effective approach is to provide constructive feedback that focuses on effort, progress, and specific strategies employed by students. By highlighting their growth and improvement, teachers encourage students to see mistakes and setbacks as valuable learning experiences.

Using growth-oriented language is another powerful tool for fostering a growth mindset in education. Teachers can emphasize the importance of effort, perseverance, and the process of learning rather than solely focusing on grades or fixed abilities. Encouraging students to view challenges as opportunities for growth and using phrases like "yet" ("I haven't mastered it yet") can instill a sense of possibility and encourage a growth mindset. Designing tasks that are challenging yet achievable, where students are encouraged to stretch beyond their comfort zones, can also foster a growth mindset by promoting resilience, problem-solving skills, and a sense of accomplishment.

By adopting these strategies and creating a classroom environment that supports growth mindset principles, educators can inspire and empower students to embrace challenges, believe in their ability to grow, and develop a lifelong love for learning.

Leadership and Organizational Culture

Leaders play a critical role in fostering a growth mindset within organizations. By cultivating a culture that values learning, encourages innovation, and embraces failure as a learning opportunity, leaders can empower their team members to develop a growth mindset. One effective strategy is to set clear expectations that emphasize growth and improvement
rather than focusing solely on immediate outcomes. Leaders can create an environment where effort, collaboration, and continuous learning are valued and rewarded.

Recognizing and celebrating effort and improvement is another important aspect of fostering a growth mindset within organizations. By acknowledging and appreciating the progress made by team members, leaders reinforce the idea that growth is valued and encouraged. Providing regular feedback that focuses on learning and development helps individuals understand how they can further enhance their skills and abilities. Leaders can also promote continuous learning and professional development opportunities, such as training programs, workshops, or mentorship initiatives, to support the growth mindset of their team members.

Creating a psychologically safe space is essential for fostering a growth mindset within organizations. When team members feel safe to take risks, share ideas, and learn from their failures, they are more likely to embrace a growth mindset. Leaders can encourage open and constructive communication, create platforms for sharing lessons learned from setbacks, and lead by example by demonstrating a growth mindset in their own actions and behaviors. By fostering a culture of psychological safety, leaders empower individuals to innovate, learn from their experiences, and contribute to the overall growth and success of the organization.

Embracing a Growth Mindset as Individuals
Individually, we have the power to foster a growth mindset in ourselves and others. By demonstrating

a growth mindset in our own actions and interactions, we inspire and influence those around us. One strategy for embracing a growth mindset is to reframe challenges as opportunities for growth and learning. Instead of seeing obstacles as insurmountable barriers, we can view them as stepping stones to progress and personal development.

Seeking opportunities for learning and growth is another powerful approach. Actively pursuing new knowledge, acquiring new skills, and seeking out challenging experiences can expand our capabilities and foster a growth mindset. By stepping outside of our comfort zones, we open ourselves up to new possibilities and embrace the joy of lifelong learning.

Supporting and encouraging others in their growth journey is also vital. By providing constructive feedback, celebrating the efforts and achievements of others, and promoting a positive and growth-oriented environment, we contribute to the development of a growth mindset in those around us. Through our support and encouragement, we inspire others to believe in their potential and embrace the mindset that they can continuously improve and achieve their goals.

By adopting these strategies and embracing a growth mindset as individuals, we not only enhance our own personal growth and development but also create a positive ripple effect that can influence and inspire those around us.

In this chapter, we explored the role of parents, teachers, leaders, and individuals in nurturing a growth mindset in others. By creating supportive environments that value effort, embrace challenges, and promote continuous learning, we empower children, students, team members, and ourselves to develop a growth mindset. Parents, teachers, and leaders can model a growth mindset, provide constructive feedback, and create environments that encourage risk-taking and learning from failures. Individually, we can embrace a growth mindset by reframing challenges, seeking continuous learning, and supporting others on their growth journey. Embracing a growth mindset not only fosters personal growth and development but also creates a positive impact on those around us. As we nurture a growth mindset in others, we contribute to a society that values effort, embraces challenges, and believes in the potential for continuous growth and improvement.

Chapter 8:

Applying the Growth Mindset in Everyday Life

In this chapter, we will discuss practical ways to apply the principles of a growth mindset in our everyday lives. By implementing the concepts and strategies covered in previous chapters, we can cultivate a mindset that fosters personal growth, resilience, and success in various areas of life.

Relationships and Communication

Having a growth mindset can greatly impact our relationships and communication with others. By approaching interactions with a growth mindset, we can foster open and constructive communication, seek understanding, and embrace opportunities for personal growth within our relationships.

One strategy for applying a growth mindset in relationships is to practice active listening. By truly listening to others without judgment or interruption, we create a safe space for open dialogue and understanding. Seeking to understand different perspectives and being open to new ideas allows us to learn and grow in our relationships. Additionally, practicing empathy and putting ourselves in others' shoes can enhance our understanding and compassion, fostering deeper connections and promoting a supportive environment.

Conflict resolution is another area where a growth mindset can be applied. Instead of avoiding conflicts or becoming defensive, we can approach disagreements with a growth-oriented perspective. By viewing conflicts as opportunities for learning and growth, we can engage in constructive conversations, find common ground, and seek resolutions that benefit everyone involved. Embracing feedback from others and being willing to reflect on our own actions and behaviors can also contribute to personal growth and strengthen our relationships.

Creating a supportive and growth-oriented environment within our relationships is essential. Encouraging and celebrating each other's growth and accomplishments, providing constructive feedback, and fostering an atmosphere where mistakes are seen as learning opportunities can cultivate a growth mindset within the relationship. By nurturing an environment that values personal development and supports each other's aspirations, we create a foundation for mutual growth and fulfillment.

Incorporating these strategies into our relationships and communication allows us to apply the principles of a growth mindset in our interactions with others. By fostering open dialogue, seeking understanding, and creating a supportive environment, we nurture stronger and more meaningful connections while promoting personal growth for ourselves and those around us.

Education and Learning

Applying a growth mindset in education and learning is key to maximizing our potential. By approaching learning with curiosity, embracing challenges, and seeking opportunities for growth, we can enhance our educational journey and develop a lifelong love for learning.

One strategy for applying a growth mindset in education is to cultivate a sense of curiosity and a thirst for knowledge. Embracing a mindset of curiosity allows us to approach new topics and subjects with enthusiasm and an open mind. By asking questions, exploring different perspectives, and seeking to understand deeper concepts, we engage in a more active and effective learning process.

Embracing challenges is another vital aspect of a growth mindset in education. Rather than shying away from difficult tasks, we can view them as opportunities to expand our abilities and knowledge. When faced with challenges, we can approach them with a positive attitude, believing in our capacity to learn and overcome obstacles. By persisting through challenges, seeking help when needed, and learning from setbacks, we develop resilience and acquire new skills and insights.

Setting goals and managing time effectively are important strategies for applying a growth mindset in education. By setting realistic and meaningful goals, we provide ourselves with a sense of direction and purpose. Break down larger goals into smaller, achievable tasks, and create a plan to work towards them. Time management skills, such as prioritizing tasks and allocating dedicated study time, help us stay focused and make progress towards our learning objectives.

Adopting a growth mindset also involves embracing a love for lifelong learning. Recognizing that learning is not limited to formal education but extends beyond the classroom allows us to seek knowledge and skills outside of traditional settings. Engaging in hobbies, attending workshops or seminars, reading books, and exploring online resources are all ways to continue our educational journey beyond academic institutions.

By applying a growth mindset in education and learning, we unlock our potential for personal growth, acquire new knowledge and skills, and develop a passion for lifelong learning. Embracing curiosity, embracing challenges, setting goals, managing time effectively, and cultivating a love for lifelong learning are all strategies that can contribute to a growth mindset in our educational pursuits.

Career and Professional Development

A growth mindset is essential for career growth and professional development. By continuously seeking learning opportunities, embracing challenges and feedback, and cultivating a mindset of adaptability and resilience, we can thrive in our professional lives.

One strategy for applying a growth mindset in our careers is to actively seek out learning opportunities. This could include attending workshops, conferences, or training programs relevant to our field. By proactively seeking new knowledge, skills, and experiences, we position ourselves for growth and advancement. Engaging in continuous learning allows us to stay current in our industry, adapt to changes, and bring new ideas and perspectives to our work.

Embracing challenges and feedback is another vital aspect of a growth mindset in our careers. Instead of shying away from difficult tasks or feedback, we can view them as opportunities for growth and improvement. Embracing challenges pushes us out of our comfort zones and allows us to develop new skills and expand our capabilities. Actively seeking feedback from colleagues, mentors, and supervisors helps us identify areas for improvement and make necessary adjustments. By using feedback constructively, we can refine our skills and enhance our performance.

Cultivating a mindset of adaptability and resilience is also crucial in our professional lives. The world of work is constantly evolving, and being adaptable to change is essential for success. A growth mindset enables us to embrace change, see it as an opportunity for growth, and pivot our skills and strategies accordingly. By cultivating resilience, we can bounce back from setbacks, learn from failures, and continue to move forward with determination and perseverance.

Setting career goals and regularly assessing our progress is another way to apply a growth mindset in our professional development. By setting meaningful goals, we provide ourselves with a sense of direction and purpose. Regularly reviewing our goals and progress allows us to make necessary adjustments and stay focused on our long-term vision. It also provides opportunities for self-reflection, celebration of achievements, and identification of areas for further growth.

By applying a growth mindset in our careers and professional development, we can unlock our potential for advancement, continuous learning, and personal fulfillment. Embracing learning opportunities, embracing challenges and feedback, cultivating adaptability and resilience, and setting career goals are strategies that contribute to a growth mindset in our professional lives.

Well-being and Personal Growth
A growth mindset is not only about achieving external success but also about personal well-being and growth. By applying a growth mindset to our self-care practices, personal development, and

overall well-being, we can enhance our resilience, self-confidence, and overall satisfaction in life.

One strategy for applying a growth mindset to well-being is to engage in regular self-reflection. Taking time to reflect on our thoughts, emotions, beliefs, and behaviors allows us to gain self-awareness and identify areas for personal growth. Through self-reflection, we can recognize our strengths, areas for improvement, and patterns that may be holding us back. By embracing self-reflection, we open ourselves up to personal growth and gain a deeper understanding of ourselves.

Self-care practices also play a crucial role in well-being and personal growth. By prioritizing self-care activities that nurture our physical, mental, and emotional well-being, we demonstrate a commitment to self-growth. Engaging in activities such as exercise, meditation, journaling, and spending
time in nature allows us to recharge, reduce stress, and cultivate a positive mindset. By making

self-care a priority, we foster a strong foundation for personal growth and well-being.

Managing setbacks and cultivating a positive mindset are key components of a growth mindset in well-being. Setbacks and challenges are inevitable in life, but it's how we respond to them that matters. By adopting a growth-oriented perspective, we can view setbacks as opportunities for learning and growth. Instead of dwelling on failures or setbacks, we can focus on the lessons learned and the steps we can take to move forward. Cultivating a positive mindset involves consciously choosing to focus on the positive aspects of our lives, practicing gratitude, and reframing negative thoughts into more empowering perspectives.

Embracing personal growth involves setting personal goals and pursuing activities that expand our horizons and challenge us. By stepping outside of our comfort zones and trying new experiences, we can stretch our capabilities and discover new strengths and interests. Engaging in lifelong learning, whether through reading, taking courses, or acquiring new skills, keeps our minds engaged and continuously stimulates personal growth.

By applying a growth mindset to our well-being and personal growth, we can enhance our resilience, self-confidence, and overall satisfaction in life. Through self-reflection, self-care practices, managing setbacks, cultivating a positive mindset, and embracing personal growth opportunities, we foster a mindset of continuous improvement and personal fulfillment.

In this chapter, we explored practical ways to apply the principles of a growth mindset in our everyday lives. By embracing a growth mindset in our relationships, education, career, and personal growth, we can unlock our full potential and experience greater fulfillment and success.

Chapter 9:

Embracing a Lifelong Growth Mindset

In this final chapter, we will summarize the key concepts and lessons covered throughout the book. By reflecting on our journey and committing to ongoing growth and development, we can unlock our full potential and lead a more fulfilling and successful life.

Key Takeaways
Throughout this book, we have explored the characteristics and impact of both fixed and growth mindsets. We have learned that a fixed mindset is characterized by the belief that our abilities and intelligence are fixed traits, while a growth mindset recognizes that these qualities can be developed through dedication, effort, and continuous learning.

In Chapter 1, we delved into the differences between the fixed mindset and the growth mindset, discussing how these mindsets influence our approach to challenges, learning, and personal development. We discovered that a fixed mindset can limit our potential, hinder our willingness to take risks, and lead to a fear of failure. On the other hand, a growth mindset encourages us to embrace challenges, persist through setbacks, and view failure as an opportunity for growth and learning.

In Chapter 2, we explored the role of beliefs in shaping our mindset. We discussed how our self-perception, self-talk, and external influences can impact our beliefs and mindset. Recognizing and challenging limiting beliefs became a key strategy for cultivating a growth mindset.

Chapter 3 emphasized the importance of embracing challenges in developing a growth mindset. We learned to reframe challenges as opportunities for growth, and we explored techniques for overcoming the fear of failure and building resilience in the face of setbacks.

In Chapter 4, we focused on cultivating resilience as an essential component of a growth mindset. We discovered strategies for bouncing back from setbacks, overcoming obstacles, and learning from failures.

Chapter 5 highlighted the significance of effort and deliberate practice in developing a growth mindset. We discussed the power of consistent effort, setting goals, and implementing effective practice strategies to enhance our skills and abilities.

In Chapter 6, we explored the value of embracing learning and seeking feedback. We recognized that a growth mindset is nurtured through continuous learning, actively seeking feedback, and viewing it as an opportunity for growth and improvement.

Chapter 7 focused on nurturing a growth mindset in others. We examined the role of parents, teachers, and leaders in fostering a growth mindset in children, students, and team members. Strategies such as creating a supportive environment, providing constructive feedback, and encouraging a growth-oriented mindset were discussed.

In Chapter 8, we explored the practical application of the growth mindset in various aspects of our lives. From relationships and communication to education and learning, and from career and professional development to well-being and personal growth, we harnessed the transformative power of the growth mindset. Embracing challenges, seeking continuous improvement, and maintaining a growth-oriented perspective allowed us to thrive and unlock our full potential. By reframing setbacks as opportunities and valuing effort, we fostered resilience and cultivated a positive impact on ourselves and those around us. As we approach the conclusion, we will recap the key insights from our journey and reiterate the value of embracing a growth mindset for ongoing personal and professional development.

Throughout these chapters, we have witnessed the transformative power of a growth mindset. We have seen how embracing a growth mindset can lead to personal growth, resilience, and success in various aspects of life. By adopting a growth mindset, we open ourselves up to new possibilities, view failures as stepping stones to success, and approach challenges with curiosity and resilience.

As we reflect on these key takeaways, let us remember that a growth mindset is not a destination, but a lifelong journey. It requires continuous effort, self-reflection, and a commitment to growth and learning. By applying the principles and strategies discussed in this book, we can cultivate a growth mindset and unlock our full potential.

Committing To Growth

Embracing a growth mindset requires more than just understanding its principles; it requires a commitment to ongoing growth and development. In this section, we will explore practical steps for cultivating and maintaining a growth mindset in our daily lives.

The first step in committing to growth is developing self-awareness. Take the time to reflect on your thoughts, beliefs, and reactions. Notice when you're exhibiting a fixed mindset and challenge those thoughts by reframing them with a growth-oriented perspective. By becoming aware of your mindset patterns, you can consciously choose to embrace a growth mindset in different areas of your life.

Challenging limiting beliefs is another important aspect of committing to growth. Identify the beliefs that hold you back and question their validity. Replace limiting beliefs with empowering ones that promote growth and possibility. Remember that you have the ability to develop new skills and improve in various areas of your life through dedicated effort and learning.

Setting growth-oriented goals is crucial for staying on the path of growth. By setting specific, measurable, achievable, relevant, and time-bound (SMART) goals, you create a roadmap for your personal and professional development. Break down your goals into smaller milestones and celebrate each achievement along the way. Regularly reassess your goals and make adjustments as needed to ensure they align with your growth mindset.

Seeking new learning opportunities is essential for maintaining a growth mindset. Keep an open mind and actively pursue avenues for learning and self-improvement. Attend workshops, take courses, read books, and engage in conversations with people who inspire and challenge you. Embrace the mindset of a lifelong learner, continuously seeking new knowledge and skills.

Persistence is key in sustaining a growth mindset. Acknowledge that growth takes time and effort. Embrace setbacks and failures as learning opportunities rather than signs of inadequacy. Persevere through challenges, even when progress seems slow. Remember that setbacks are not roadblocks but detours on the path to growth.

By committing to growth, you create a mindset of continuous improvement and development. Embrace self-awareness, challenge limiting beliefs, set growth-oriented goals, seek new learning opportunities, and persist through obstacles. It is through this commitment and daily practice that a growth mindset becomes ingrained in your way of thinking and living.

Sustaining Motivation and Accountability
Maintaining motivation and accountability are essential for sustaining a growth mindset throughout your journey. In this section, we will discuss strategies for staying motivated, managing setbacks, and holding yourself accountable for your growth.

One strategy for sustaining motivation is to create a positive support system. Surround yourself with individuals who uplift and inspire you. Seek out mentors, friends, or colleagues who embody a growth mindset and can provide guidance and encouragement along your journey. Engage in communities or join groups that share your growth-oriented values. Connecting with like-minded individuals can boost your motivation and provide valuable support.

Managing setbacks is an inevitable part of any growth journey. When faced with obstacles or failures, it's important to remember that setbacks are not permanent. Reframe setbacks as opportunities for learning and growth. Analyze what went wrong, extract lessons from the experience, and apply those lessons moving forward. Embrace resilience and use setbacks as stepping stones to further development.

Accountability plays a vital role in sustaining a growth mindset. Create mechanisms that hold you accountable for your growth goals. This could be through accountability partnerships, where you check in with a trusted friend or colleague regularly to discuss progress and challenges. Alternatively, you can establish personal accountability systems, such as tracking your progress in a journal or using apps that help you stay focused on your goals. Find the method that works best for you and commit to staying accountable.

Celebrating milestones along your growth journey is crucial for maintaining motivation. Acknowledge and reward yourself for the progress you've made. Celebrate even the small wins as they are stepping stones towards your larger goals. This recognition and celebration will fuel your motivation and inspire you to keep pushing forward.

Motivation can come from both intrinsic and extrinsic sources. While intrinsic motivation, such as personal fulfillment and passion for growth, is powerful, don't overlook the value of external motivation. Set up incentives or rewards for reaching milestones. These can serve as additional boosts to keep you motivated and excited about your growth journey.

By staying motivated and holding yourself accountable, you cultivate a growth mindset that persists through challenges and propels you forward. Remember to nurture your support system, manage setbacks with resilience, and celebrate your progress along the way. With sustained motivation and accountability, you will continue to embrace the transformative power of a growth mindset.

Embracing the Journey

Embracing a lifelong growth mindset is not a destination but a continuous journey. In this section, we will reflect on the transformative power of a growth mindset and encourage you to embrace the ups and downs of your growth journey. We will emphasize the importance of resilience, self-compassion, and embracing change as we navigate through life's challenges. By viewing setbacks as learning opportunities and celebrating our successes, we can fully embrace the growth mindset journey and experience personal and professional growth along the way.

The growth mindset journey is not always easy. There will be obstacles, doubts, and moments of uncertainty. But it is through these challenges that we have the opportunity to grow and develop. Embrace resilience in the face of adversity, knowing that setbacks are not indicative of your worth or abilities. Cultivate self-compassion, offering kindness and understanding to yourself when faced with difficulties. Treat yourself with the same compassion and encouragement you would extend to a friend on their growth journey.

Embracing change is another crucial aspect of the growth mindset journey. The world around us is constantly evolving, and by embracing change, we open ourselves up to new possibilities and opportunities for growth. Let go of the fear of the unknown and approach change with curiosity and an open mind. Adaptability and flexibility are key qualities that will support your growth and help you thrive in an ever-changing world.

As you embark on this growth mindset journey, remember that it is not a race or a competition. Each individual's journey is unique, and progress may look different for each person. Celebrate your own growth and the growth of others, knowing that we are all on our own paths toward personal and professional development.

Conclusion

In this book, we have explored the significance of mindsets and the transformative power of adopting a growth mindset. We have dived into the characteristics of a fixed mindset and a growth mindset, understanding how they shape our thoughts, behaviors, and outcomes.

Throughout each chapter, we have examined the role of beliefs, challenges, resilience, effort, learning, and nurturing a growth mindset in various aspects of life. We have provided practical strategies and techniques to cultivate and maintain a growth mindset, emphasizing the importance of self-awareness, self-reflection, and ongoing commitment to growth.

As we conclude this book, I hope that you have gained valuable insights and tools to embrace a growth mindset in your personal and professional life. Embrace the key takeaways, commit to growth, and sustain motivation and accountability. Embrace the journey with resilience, self-compassion, and a willingness to adapt to change.

Remember, the growth mindset journey is a lifelong one. Embrace the ups and downs, view setbacks as opportunities for growth, and celebrate your progress along the way. By cultivating a growth mindset, you unlock your full potential, tap into your inner strength, and experience personal and professional growth beyond your imagination.

Thank you for joining me on this enlightening exploration of mindsets and the transformative power of a growth mindset. May your journey be filled with continuous growth, resilience, and a passion for lifelong learning.

Made in the USA
Las Vegas, NV
10 August 2023

75652719R00050